The Art of My Reality

The Art of My Reality

A Poetic Memoir

VONDELL M. CARTHRAN

To my Wife, I say Thank You.

It was your encouragement, faith in me, and belief in my abilities, that made this book happen. You encouraged me to turn my childhood dream into a reality. You have been my staunchest supporter. You have been my confidant, my editor, my proofreader, my critic, and my cheerleader. Even though most of my poems were written before I met you, this book is a better book because of You. Thank you Honey.

TABLE OF CONTENTS

PREFACE

This book is a compilation of my poetry throughout the years. It is not a complete collection of my work. For various reasons, over time I neglected to save everything that I had written. These are the poems that have survived my multiple moves, relocations, house cleanings, and memory losses.

My poetry is demonstrative of my mental state at the time of the writings. My highs, lows, and emotions on the selected topics. I have dated the poems and noted my age. Hoping to provide you a glimpse into my personality, at that particular moment.

Poetry is personal and expressive. It is a mechanism to relay your thoughts on a subject or an emotion. My poems were inspired by the events of my life. It was a way to release my joys and my tears. A way of venting and of sharing. It was my way of telling the world what I was thinking.

In this collection, you will find that I have an old school style of writing. I enjoy rhymes and the art of using them to convey a message. True art will evoke an emotional response from the observer. Art speaks to each person differently. There is no right or wrong interpretation. There is only the Art and how you perceive it for yourself.

1

PROLOGUE

August 1980, I was 20 years old. I wrote this while the country was dealing with a serial killer in Atlanta, Georgia. From July 1979 to May 1981, Wayne Williams murdered at least 28 children, adolescents, and adults. He was arrested June 21, 1981, and is serving a life sentence.

When I wrote this, Black children were being killed but no one knew by whom or why.

Have Faith

Here we are enjoying life, partying right alone,
Walking around with gleeful faces as if nothing is going wrong;
But the world goes on outside of these petrified walls,
We stand back in horror as children in Atlanta fall;

Children with hopes and ambitions, waiting for that fulfilling day,
Yet because of a bloodthirsty maniac, their dreams are wiped away;
Jesus said, "blessed are the meek for they shall inherit the earth,"
How can they claim their inheritance, if their bodies lie under dirt;

Lord help us to understand that which is concealed from the eye,
What is the purpose of such actions, why must innocent children die;
People of Atlanta, we offer you our condolences and our heartfelt prayers,
Things we hope will comfort you in your hours of despair;

I would like to personally offer some time-tested advice,
Have faith in the world and keep God in charge of your life;
Show the joy for life that we were all put here to display,
Always remember that Jesus, is the truth, the power, the light, and the way.

2

PROLOGUE

It was Sunday. January 11, 1981. It was a difficult time for me. I was 20 years old and felt like I was not progressing in my life. I had dreamt of the NFL since I was 12 years old. I wasn't ready to give up that dream.

I wrote this after I had given up my apartment, returned to live at my mother's house, and formulated my plan to get into college.

Dreamers

Perhaps I am just a foolish dreamer.
Yet, was not the world made productive by such dreamers?
Individuals that, by keeping their hopes and ambitions alive, have made this planet a better place for us all.

Dreams without ambitions are fantasies.
Ambition without hope is fruitless.
It is preposterous to think that one can be accomplished without the other.

Dreamers are initially considered insane.
Once their dreams are transformed into reality, they are labeled as brilliant.
Woe the price the dreamer must pay.

If not for dreamers, there would be no accomplishments.
Without accomplishments, there would be no progress.
Without progress, there would be no human race.
Continue to hope, continue to dream. It is the first step to Success.

3

PROLOGUE

It was the summer of 1980. I was 20 years old. I had just moved back to Griertown in an attempt to restructure my life. I met a girl from South Carolina named Angela. She was a very attractive young lady and we had a lot of fun together. It was a three month romance but it never got intimate. She went back home at the end of the summer and I never saw her again.

I wrote her this poem before she left.

MY ANGEL

There once was an angel of beauty, her smile did the whole world enjoy,
She enhanced the earth like rays of sunshine, her presence could not be ignored;
Her beauty, it was beyond comprehension, it's believed to have saved many men,
Those with lonely, desolate lives, dearly in need of a friend;

She would come into their world, and open up their heart,
Show them the splendor of peace, and describe life as a delicate art;
She would teach them the meaning of love, and all the treasures it brings,
Some men called her the Goddess of Love, while others called her the Queen;

She possessed a smile of joy, with a warmth that could melt the soul,
For centuries, men searched emphatically for her, until their bodies grew tired and old;
It is said that such an angel is a myth, and could not possibly be true,
However those must be the words of a madman, for I have found that Angel, in You.

4

Prologue

November 1982. I was 22 years old. Home from college for the Thanksgiving holiday. My new life is looking great. There were roughly 100 students that tried out for the football team at North Carolina Central University. I was one of two regular students to make the team. My classes were going well. College was challenging but exciting. I was thankful for the good and the bad.

THANKSGIVING PRAYER

Our Heavenly Father . . .
We thank thee for the friends thou has blessed us with,
For each is a part of us, that we cherish as thy precious gift;
We thank thee for our enemies, that seek to do us harm,
For they remind us of the evils we will encounter, as life does carry on;

We thank thee for our loved ones, and those that we have pleased,
For they are the ones that share our victories, our happiness, and our glee;
We thank thee for the drink of life, that we thirst for day by day,
For the power to make it sweeter, in each and every way;

We thank thee for the small things in life, that men think little of,
For these are your gifts to us, that we relish most and love;
We thank thee for our peace of mind, our honesty, and our health,
For these are the treasures one should seek in life, not popularity or wealth;

O Glorious Father, bless us on this your Thanksgiving Day,
Show us what is truly important, the truth, the light, and the way.

Let all of God's children say Amen.

5

PROLOGUE

The date was June 1985. I was 25 years old. I was living in Durham, North Carolina, and driving a truck for the Coca Cola Company. I was waiting to join the Air Force in December.

I really don't know why I wrote this. It was just one of those days. I'm not even sure if it was raining outside. But it was definitely raining inside of me.

It Rains In Black

Some days are gloom and dreary. Days when the sun is shining but it rains in black. A black that paints the earth as though some hand was artistically engineering it. My mind grows bewildered and my behavior shows the strain of being unable to understand. *It rains in black only where I tread.*

Everything is soaked in darkness. Droplets of water hang from the trees like black blood. The foliage that was once bright and radiant, now gleam of death. Beautiful flora that once sparked happiness, now leans to the ground drenched in murky fluids. *It rains in black only where I tread.*

Why does the Creator burden me with such days? The earth is smiling while my world is in tears. Babies are born, while the child inside of me dies. But I shall not give up. I shall move forward. I will succeed. Through the rain, I can see the sun. *It rains in black only where I tread.*

6

PROLOGUE

I wrote this on Sunday, June 30, 1985. I was 25 years old. I don't remember the motivation for writing it. Knowing me, I probably saw something about a boy and a dog that made me think about the dog's perspective. Naturally I had to put it into words.

A Dog And His Boy

It's so hard to describe how beautiful the earth truly is. When I speak of beauty I don't mean the arrangements of colors, or the amount of diversities. I refer to the complexity of its existence and the simplistic realization of its eventual death.

I have lived a modest life. I have dedicated myself to exploring and learning. I will delve into any hole in my search for knowledge. You see, I believe in truth and realities. The elements that are prerequisites for wisdom.

Mankind knows nothing of wisdom. They spend their existence, seven times that of mine, searching and destroying. They claim to seek knowledge, yet they kill anything that they do not understand. Such a pitiful, shameless race.

Look at him, sitting there asleep. A whole world of knowledge to explore and there he is wearing that stupid hat, no shoes on his tender little feet, holding a stick attached to a string and hook in the water . . . asleep! And to top things off, he doesn't eat fish. He hates it!!! Such a silly race.

And here I am, in my declining years, tied to a freaking tree. I would rather be imprisoned than to be enslaved. With freedom so close yet unreachable. All things considered though . . . I'm happy. I've accepted my lot in life. It's been a good life. He's a good boy and he has a good heart. I've taught him a lot and he's learned it well. He's MY boy.

7

Prologue

The date was September 12, 1985. It was a Thursday. I had left Durham and returned to Charlotte, North Carolina, in preparation for my entry into the U.S. Air Force.

I was driving a Coke truck and working part-time at Arby's, while in Durham. In Charlotte, I did temp work to pay the bills. I had three months before going to basic training.

It was fall and the football season had just started. I could hear the "Call of the Wild" in my head. I could smell the grass of the football field. I could feel the excitement of battle in my heart. But that was no longer my journey.

My path now led to the military. I went from playing a sport, to protecting the country. I was 25 years old and had been playing football for most of my life. Now I was switching trains and not sure exactly where this one was headed. I was desperately missing football.

No More

I have played my last football game. Never again will I hear the cheers of thousands of fans. Never again will I have that confident feeling of knowing that I had given my best.

Through the years, I have known many thrills, as well as many pains. I have constantly pushed my body to its limit. I have had dislocations, fractures, and broken bones. I have put my body and my life at risk to play a game.

But I have no regrets. Football has given me confidence and morality. It has taught me to always give my best and to never give up. Through football I have learned to cherish my body and respect my abilities. I have learned teamwork, I have learned self-pride, and I have learned dedication. Yet, the most important lesson I have learned is to go beyond my potential. To go farther than I think I am capable.

Football is over but my life has just begun. Football has taken me places that I could not have reached by any other means. Now I must rely on my intelligence and not my body. Now I must follow the path of reality and not that of dreams.

8

PROLOGUE

It was 8:56 p.m. on Friday, January the 3, 1986. I was 25 years old. I was in Basic Training at Lackland Air Force Base. I had left college early and completely changed my life by joining the military.

I was excited, yet apprehensive. I needed something in my life that was stable and secure. I wasn't sure about joining the military but I knew I had to do something.

These are my thoughts that night, as I sat on my bunk preparing for Lights Out. I was exhausted, stressed, and uncertain. It had been a long time since I had put my thoughts into the written word.

So I grabbed my pad and pen. I wrote the first thoughts that came into my head regarding how I felt about my new life.

New Beginning

I've traveled down a rocky road, that has led me neither here nor there,
I've had many wondrous dreams that have vanished into thin air;
I've done a lot of petty things, for which I am not proud,
I've hidden myself within a shell, to stay away from the crowd;

I've lived my life as I've seen fit, doing only what I choose,
I've always had a positive mind, knowing that I could never lose;
I've tried to be a good human being, believing in right and wrong,
I've traveled through the thorns of life, but never for very long;

I've come here to this Place of Lies, searching for success,
I shall leave here still in search, yet able to confess;
I've never tried with all my heart, to give life all I had,
I've never tried my very best, and for that I am truly sad;

Now my life has turned around, though my direction is not clear,
I know that if I follow my plans, failure I need not fear;
The day will come when I shall leave this place, and a world of old behind,
All the riches I seek in life, I promise will be mine.

9

PROLOGUE

The date was May of 1987. My age is 27. I was in Tech school at Goodfellow AFB, San Angelo, Texas. It's my birthday month. Tech school was a good time in my life. I matured a lot and I accomplished even more. I was very proud of myself.

I don't know what prompted me to write this. Apparently someone must have pissed me off. 😊

MOVE FIRST HIMSELF

You come, you observe, you opinionate
– Let he who would move the world, move first himself.

You speak of wisdom, yet you act of ignorance
– Let he who would move the world, move first himself.

You would build mountains, yet you stumble over pebbles
– Let he who would move the world, move first himself.

You dare have the audacity to tell me how I should better my life
– Let he who would move the world, move first himself.

10

PROLOGUE

Circa 1988, 28 years old. I was happy and in love. I wrote this for my then girlfriend but I never gave it to her. I don't really know why. But I'm glad I saved it and I'm glad I married her. We've been together for 34 years and counting.

HAPPINESS

Happiness is a word, often hard to express,
It's that smile on your face, that's impossible to suppress;
Happiness is an emotion that brings one great joy,
Like the first explorations of a girl discovering a boy;

Happiness is love, they are one and the same,
They are words we all know, words I need not explain;
You are my Happiness, the pride of my life,
You are my best friend, and one day my Wife.

11

PROLOGUE

It was the winter of 1999. I was 39 years old. I was in Charlotte caring for my ailing mother. Little did I know it would be the last winter I would spend with her. I was sitting in my childhood bedroom, thinking about being back home in the hood. My mind replayed the events of my youth and the lessons that it had taught me.

The Ghetto

In the ghetto, one experiences many things,
Violence, death, and the loss of dreams;
Each day is worse than the one before,
Searching for crumbs and begging for more;

As children, we didn't notice the dirt or the crime,
Our focus was play, our only limit was time;
As teenagers, we found a world that was unfair,
Confusing and heartless, in need of repair;

As young adults came the choice, the crossroad of life,
Prosperity to the left, incarceration to the right;
Ghetto life is hard, it can break your spirit,
It can crush your dreams, but you need not fear it;

Believe in yourself and develop a plan,
Trust in your vision, believe that you can;
Lean on your family, love will show you the way,
Listen to your elders, and heed what they have to say;
In the ghetto, one experiences many things,
Learning from those experiences, will make you a King.

12

Prologue

I wrote this in June of 2000. I was 40 years old. This was a collaboration with my wife. It was the first and only time I have ever collaborated with someone on a poem. We wrote it for my mother's funeral. She wrote the first half and I did the second half. I think we made a great team.

Welcome Home

You sought the Word,
Now you've found the Word;
You studied the Word,
Now you know the Word;
You've endured a great deal of pain,
But you stayed true to the Word;

It was a long and courageous battle,
You may take your place at the foot of the throne;
Your earthly struggles are no more,
Welcome home, thy good and faithful servant;
Let Heaven rejoice and Satan tremble,
Another Angel has joined the army of God.

PROLOGUE

Circa 2010. I was 50 years old. I'm not sure about the motivation for this piece. All I know is that it originally started out as a veiled attempt to write a song. However, I am not musically inclined, nor am I a lyricist. So I decided to stay in my lane and do what I do best.

We are One

Hold your head up high,
Be so proud you can touch the sky,
Don't let the fool hold you down;

Be all that you can,
We are products of Kings and Queens my friend,
We've got to show the world that we are one;

For 400 years, we have lived in a world of hate and fear,
Running, hiding, barely surviving,
Remaining alive by destroying our pride,

Once we had the freedom to roam,
Now we're a people without a home,
We've got to show the world that we are one;

We assemble together hand in hand,
Shunned by the ancestors of our native land,
Feet planted firmly on the ground that we stand;

Finding strength in our camaraderie,
As we continue to form our own identity,
We've got to show the world that we are one.

14

PROLOGUE

May 23, 2010. I am 50 years old. In this historic year of living a half century, I reflect back on my life. I think about my childhood, my birth family, my friends, my accomplishments, my wife, and my kids. Ah, my kids…the best part of me.

The day they were born are two special days. My daughter was born between Christmas and New Year. My son was born on the Fourth of July at 12 noon. I remember each birth vividly. I remember looking at them for the first time. I remember how I felt as I welcomed them into the world.

Chalese and Marquette, you are my greatest joys, my greatest accomplishments, my greatest blessings.

My Kids

Christmas has passed and a new year looms,
I look in your eyes and my heart is consumed;
My smile, my joy, the gleam in my eyes,
Are all signs of love and a heart filled with pride;
Here lies my daughter, my cherished first born,
I will love you forever, on this I have sworn.

It's the 4th of July, the sun is high noon,
I could sense his greatness, as his voice filled the room;
He's my little man, the bearer of my name,
A version of myself, a keeper of the flame;
I want to shout to the world, across the seven seas,
Behold my son, in whom I am well pleased.

My kids are my joy, the blessings of my life,
The reason I live, the reason I fight;
They give me purpose, they complete my soul,
They fill my void, they make me whole;
I thank God for this life, and all that they add,
I thank God for the gift, of being their Dad.

15

PROLOGUE

I wrote this circa 2016. I am 56 years old. Just sitting at work, thinking about my best friend. I wanted her to know how much I love her so I put this on Facebook as a tribute. We have a long history. I have known her entire family for many years. She has been there through every facet of my life. This was a way of expressing my affection for her. I'm really proud of this piece.

BEST FRIENDS

This morning I woke and thought about my best friend in the whole wide world, Janice Clay. I thought about all the years we have been friends. I thought about all the great times we've had growing up in Griertown. I've thought about the memories we have going back to junior high school. I thought about how much I genuinely love her and I know that she genuinely loves me. She is my heart, my joy, and my inspiration. I am blessed by God to have her as a part of my life. She is a member of my family. She is my Sister and I am her Brother. I would die for her.

If there is someone on your mind that you feel pure love for, then let them know. Reach out and touch their heart. We get caught up with our daily activities and take our loved ones for granted. Especially the ones that we seldom get to see. Let them know that they are special to your life and you haven't forgotten about them.

Janice, I love you. Thank you for being my friend.

16

PROLOGUE

It was February 26, 2021. I was 60 years old. My oldest sister, Deanie Carthran, had written a poem in tribute to our mother. It is a beautiful piece and she has given me permission to include it in my book. Our mother was the matriarch of our family. Her passing left a void in all our lives that can never be filled. She was strong, loving, caring, independent, and reliable. She was the epitome of what a Mother and Grandmother should be.

Myrtis Burton Carthran. 11/28/37–6/16/2000

ACCEPTANCE

June 16, 2000, was the day that our Savior had you taken away.

I felt a hollow feeling inside, for weeks, for months,

I cried and cried. Deep down I felt that I too, had died.

I sank deep into depression.

I felt so alone. I prayed to God to also call me home.

I asked God to hear my plea, to reunite my mother and me.

He answered my call, but in a different way.

He showed me that I'd see you again someday.

He helped me accept what I could not change,

And to find solemn and relief through the grief and the pain.

I love and miss you mama,

Deanie

17

Prologue

March 10, 2021. I was 60 years old. I've always wanted to write something for my boys, Curbeam and D.S. They know how I feel about them but, like most men, it often goes unsaid. So here's my tribute to my lifelong friends . . . to my Brothers.

MY BROTHERS

We've been together most of our lives,
We've done things bad and good;
We've always had each other's back,
That's how you grow up in the hood;

Girls, sports, fights after school,
Making money the best way you can;
Doing things that you know are wrong,
Trying to prove you're a man;

We've always been there for each other,
In times of laughter and in times of tears;
We love each other without judgment,
We trust each other without fear;

We are family in many ways,
My two brothers and I;
Three friends forever connected,
By a bond we can never deny.

18

PROLOGUE

It was March 22, 2021. I was 60 years old. We recently had an insurrection on the nation's Capitol. The violent coup attempt was sparked by the 45th President of the United States. The election of 2020 removed him from office. In the aftermath, I've never seen the country this divided. I've never seen this much hatred and uncertainty. I don't know how to fix it, but teaching our kids how to love everyone is a great starting point.

One Race

When a child is born, it has no prejudice,
Every sight is amazing, every sound melodious;
When a child is born, it learns at a rapid rate,
Determining good from bad, love from hate;

Children at the park will play all day long,
Filling their minds with games, and the air with song;
Their hearts beating with joy, swing sets in the air,
New friendships formed, some started on a dare;

They go to school with thoughts unchained,
Learning letters, numbers, colors, and names;
They learn of people all over the world,
Some have straight hair and some rock a curl;

It's not our differences that keep us apart,
It's the amount of love that we have in our heart;
We should teach our children to be good and be true,
To be accepting of others that look different than you;

Let children be children, leave them alone,
Teach them to love, allow their minds to roam;
Show them that the world is a beautiful place,
We are all one people, we are all one Race.

19

PROLOGUE

It was March 31, 2021. I was 60 years old. My childhood friends and I often talk about the good old days. I love conversations, movies, and songs that reminisce about days gone by. One such song is "Back In The Day" by Ahmad. It reminds me of my childhood experiences. I used the hook to that song to help me tell my story.

Back In The Day

"Back in the day when I was young, I'm not a kid anymore, but some days I sit and wish I was a kid again."

Growing up we ate bologna (cold or fried), peanut butter and jelly, grilled cheese sandwiches, and pork-n-beans with hot dogs. We also ate hamburgers and hot dogs on loaf bread, and all we drank was Kool-Aid.

We made ice cream using condensed milk, ice, and rock salt. We had home-cooked dinners almost every night except for Saturday. That's when it was every man for himself.

There was only one TV. Our mother called us from another room to come and turn the channel. Usually with a pair of pliers because the knob was broken.

We took our school clothes off as soon as we got home and put on our play clothes. We walked to and from school. During those walks, we played kissing games, got into fights, joked with one another, and made after-homework plans.

We played Freeze Tag, Red Light/Green Light, Rolling Bat, Hopscotch, Hide and Seek, Truth or Dare, and Dodgeball. We roller skated, rode bikes all over the neighborhood and to the other side of town. There was no bottled water. We drank from the tap and the water hose. When someone had a fight, that's all it was and we were friends again the next day.

There were no cell phones. If your mother wanted you, she told one of your friends and they hunted you down. We watched our mouths around our elders and didn't talk while "grown folks were talking." We were taught to stay in a child's place.

Those were the good old days. I loved growing up in Griertown. It was a great time!!!

"Back in the day when I was young, I'm not a kid anymore, but some days I sit and wish I was a kid again."

20

Quotes

Bravery is not the absence of fear, it is the mastery
over it. (Paraphrase of Mark Twain)

The best thing a father can do for his children,
is to love their mother. (By Many)

It is an honor to raise another human being. You are blessed,
if you have that privilege. (Vondell M. Carthran)

When you come to the end of your rope, tie a knot
in it and hold on. (Franklin D. Roosevelt)

No matter the odds, I will, I shall, I must. (Vondell M. Carthran)

God bless me as I try to bless others. (Vondell M. Carthran)

Patience is the road by which ambition travels
to success. (Paraphrase of Bill Bradley)

You know what you have to do. The choice is
yours to do it. (Vondell M. Carthran)

Behold my Son, in whom I am well pleased.
(Alex Haley, *Roots*)

21

SHORT TAKES

God is my silent partner. He wants me to succeed. I am not destined, for no one is. But my silent partner is rooting for me. He has given me everything I need to be happy. The decision is mine. I decide what is important. I decide if there is joy in my heart. I decide if I will let you steal that joy. (Vondell M. Carthran)

The European slave trade was an African man stepping out of his hut for a breath of fresh air. Then four months later, ending up in South Carolina with lashes on his back and a brand on his chest. (Vondell M. Carthran)

Slavery in America was a Black mother suffocating her newborn baby, because she didn't want it to grow up a slave. (By many Historians)

It is a hard task to keep a dream alive. Believe in yourself and others will believe in you too. Keep the faith, for that which you think becomes your world. (Vondell M. Carthran)

The wind blew wildly across the great plain,
The animals shivered beneath the hardened rain;
There were thousands of bullets once called sand,
It was beauty yet deadly, this funnel on land. (Vondell M. Carthran)

If loyalty is an important element in all relationships,
And a woman is man's most perfect partner,
Why is a dog his most loyal companion? (Vondell M. Carthran)

www.ingramcontent.com/pod-product-compliance
Lightning Source LLC
Chambersburg PA
CBHW031637170726
47990CB00017B/1431